Birds

Copyright © 1988, Raintree Publishers Inc.

Translated by Hess-Inglin Translation Services

Library of Congress Number: 87-28786

2 3 4 5 6 7 8 9 0   91 90 89 88

Printed and bound in the United States of America.

Library of Congress Cataloging in Publication Data

Birds.

  (Science and its secrets)
  Includes index.
  Summary: Describes the physical characteristics, habits, and
natural environment of various species of birds.
  1. Birds—Juvenile literature.   [1. Birds]
I. Series.
QL676.2.B57   1988   598   87-28786
ISBN 0-8172-3084-X (lib. bdg.)
ISBN 0-8172-3090-4 (softcover)

BIRDS

Raintree Publishers — Milwaukee

Contents

What is a bird?

When you think about birds, you immediately think of an animal that flies. However, not all birds fly, and some other animals have this ability. Insects or even mammals such as bats, for example, can fly. But birds do have several characteristics which set them apart from other animals.

For one thing, birds belong to the only class of animals that have feathers. Birds developed feathers millions of years ago. Feathers, identical to those of modern birds, covered the body of archaeopteryx 160 million years ago. This animal is the oldest bird known today. However, archaeopteryx still shared many characteristics with its reptile relatives. For example, it had both teeth and a long, bony tail. The wings of this bird were about the size of a magpie's. These wings were only for soaring. They were not powerful enough to allow it to fly freely up into the sky. Today, some bird species are born completely naked. But, of course, they soon grow feathers.

The bird's wings are also unique. The change from front limbs to wings also changed the bird's skeleton. Most birds now have a very specialized skeleton with hollow bones. These hollow bones decrease the bird's weight. This makes its flight easier. However, birds whose bones must withstand frequent shocks are different. For example, most of the skull bones of the woodpecker are not hollow. This is probably so because they so vigorously strike trees with their beaks.

Birds, like mammals, are also warm-blooded. All other classes of animals must adapt to the surrounding temperature. Animals such as reptiles, insects, mollusks, etc., must adapt or die.

Among birds, there are some characteristics common to all. For example, all birds have beaks. Often a beak is used not only for eating, but also as a tool. Also, all birds reproduce by laying eggs. These line up one after the other in the body of the female. (This is very different from reptiles, for example, which may lay hundreds or even thousands of eggs at once.) But aside from these, bird species are very different from one another. Characteristics such as habits, diets, and environments vary from bird to bird.

The archaeopteryx is known as the first bird. From fossilized remains, scientists think it must have looked something like this.

Why are feathers important?

Birds' feathers have several functions. Because they meet different needs, feathers can have several forms. Basically, feathers stick out of the bird's skin, like mammals' hair. They are made of a more or less rigid shaft, called the rachis. This shaft has many barbs on it. The barbs give form to the feather. If you look closely, you can see that these barbs have much tinier barbs. The tiny barbs are called barbules. The barbules are a kind of hair. They act like tiny hooks and grab onto each other. This gives the feather a smooth, even appearance.

The feathers themselves are called contour feathers. Together, all of the bird's feathers are known as its plumage. Some of them are used for flying. Feathers known as wing primaries and tail feathers are two examples. Others protect the bird's body, especially on the back and on the fleshy part of the wings. These are called covert feathers. They are generally rigid, and their barbs are very tightly knit.

Feathers known as "down" are not held together by barbs. Many young birds are born covered by these soft, fluffy feathers. This down keeps them warm. In some species, like sea gulls, the chicks' down is speckled and helps camouflage them. But adult birds have down, too. In adults, though, the down is usually hidden by the contour feathers. There it serves as insulation from the cold. Between the down and the contour feathers, there are often intermediary feathers. These feathers have tips that resemble contour feathers and bases that are downy. These feathers serve two functions at once.

It is also necessary to mention the filose feathers. These feathers can be compared to hair, since they do not have barbs. They can be seen on the bodies of plucked birds. Their function is not known for certain. But they seem to separate the males and females of some species.

The vibrissae are bristly feathers. They look like moustaches and serve as a sense organ in many birds. In the owl, for example, they are found around the beak. Owls tend to be short-sighted, so the vibrassae make up for this. They give the owl a "sense of touch" that help it find its prey.

On the flight feathers, the barbules are tightly attached to each other.

After about fifteen days, the down on young birds of prey is replaced by real feathers. Birds of prey are those that hunt and kill animals for their food.

The cormorant is often seen perched in the sunshine with its wings spread. Experts think the bird does this to quickly dry its feathers.

How do birds become waterproof?

The heron uses a special dust to protect itself against moisture. This dust is made from a special down on the bird's breast.

When a duck comes out of the water, excess water flows down its plumage without wetting it. Even young sea gulls come out of the water barely wet. This is so even when they are still only covered by down. But if you find a feather and soak it in water, it usually winds up in sad shape.

The answer is simple. Birds protect their feathers against the water and rain by waterproofing them. This is done with an oil substance produced by a gland known as the uropygial or preening gland. This gland is located at the base of the bird's tail. Birds take oil from this gland with their beaks. They then coat their plumages with it.

This waterproofing operation is generally done before a very complete washing. Some birds even take an "ant bath" beforehand. First a bird allows ants to crawl into its plumage by laying down in an anthill. As they crawl through the bird's feathers, the ants deposit a substance called formic acid. Formic acid is a colorless, strong-smelling liquid given off by the ants. In the bird's feathers, it acts as a repellent for many parasites.

Some birds, such as the ostrich, do not have preening glands. On herons they are very small. This wader, in fact, has another way of waterproofing. On its breast, the heron has layers of special down which decompose into a fine dust. The bird coats its plumage, then smoothes and cleans it. This is done with one of the bird's toes. This special toe has a comb just for this function. The dust of the down, being greasy, is almost enough to waterproof the bird. Only a small amount of oil from the preening gland is added .

Strangely, all birds do not know how to waterproof themselves properly. Cormorants, for example, often leave the water with their feathers partially wet. After that they are often seen perched on a buoy with their wings spread open. Experts think that this is how the bird dries itself.

In some ways, this waterproofing is very sensitive. Pollution, especially oil products left behind by the oil tankers, destroys the waterproof coating. Even just a spot of it on a bird's feathers allows water to seep beneath the contour feathers. Then it soaks the down, and the bird loses its insulating layer. In this condition, a bird could die of cold in a few hours.

The male hornbill imprisons his mate in the hollow of a tree during the nesting period. The female then molts all at once as she sits on her eggs.

What happens to feathers when they are worn out?

You can see that a bird's plumage is very important to its survival. Despite the care given them, feathers still become worn. They sometimes break and must be renewed.

Periodically, the bird's internal mechanisms cast off its old feathers. This is called molting. During this time, the bird's worn feathers fall out by themselves. They are then replaced by quills. The quill is the lower part of the feather's shaft. This will grow to include the rachis of a new feather. Normally, the inside of these stems are filled with dead matter. But during this time, they are filled with blood vessels. The vessels will carry materials necessary for the formation of barbs.

Most birds molt at least once a year. Often they molt at the end of the mating season. Some males grow a very showy plumage during mating season to attract the females. At the end of mating season, this is no longer needed. Birds, such as ducks, then take on a less colorful plumage called an eclipse plumage. Another partial molt will renew all of their beauty at the beginning of the winter.

Other birds molt at different times. Swallows wait until the end of their migration to molt. They do not have time to change feathers before that. The ptarmigan changes plumage three times each year. This allows the bird to blend into the season's landscape, sometimes snowy, sometimes flowered.

Many birds molt a little at a time.

Their feathers fall one by one from each side. This allows the bird to keep its balance during flight. Ducks, geese, and swans, on the contrary, lose all of their primary feathers at once. Then they cannot fly for a period lasting from fifteen days up to one and a half months. During this time, they gather in deserted areas where they will be safe.

The male hornbill closes the female in the hollow of a tree during nest building. The male walls up the hollow with dry earth, leaving just a small hole for her beak. He then feeds her through this hole. The female hornbill takes this time to molt all at once. While in her prison, she has almost no feathers.

The molt is not the only cause of color change in a bird. Some feathers are a different color at the tip than at the base. This is caused by wear. As the tip of the feather wears away, the bird seems to change color.

African birds known as touracos owe their beautiful colors to special pigments . . .

. . . while starlings owe their color to iridescence.

What causes birds' vivid colors?

Certain birds are noted for the beauty and colors of their plumage. But what is most remarkable is the process used by nature to produce these colors. Some colors are produced by substances called pigments. These pigments give birds color just like they give color to mammals' coats. One of the most common pigments is melanin. Melanin is a dark pigment which gives blackbirds and crows their appearance.

The red tints are often caused by a substance with a carotene base. This substance is found in all plants having chlorophyll. Birds do not make this substance themselves, but they find it in their food. For example, pink flamingoes find it in the microscopic algae and small shell fish that they eat. Sometimes flamingoes are not given the right food in zoos. Then they lose their beautiful colors and become drab. In the same way, canary breeders know that a bird's color is often related to its diet. They color their birds pink by giving them paprika. This spice contains a pigment of the color pink.

But pigments are not the only cause of bright colors in birds. Some tints are caused by the structure of the bird's feathers. The different structures absorb certain wavelengths of light and reflect the others toward an observer's eye. The color of the feathers having this structure changes according to whether they are observed in reflected light or direct light.

In some cases the tints produced in this way may be iridescent. This means that they change color according to the angle from which they are seen. This is true of birds such as starlings and blackbirds. This is caused by certain barbules that no longer have their hooklets. That is why this iridescence is never seen on flight feathers. The barbs must stay tightly spaced in order to support the bird.

Finally, some tints are caused by external coloring. This is true of the white pelican. During mating season, this bird takes on a pink tint. It gets its color from the oil secreted by its preening gland at this time.

When it comes to beauty, the bird of paradise has no competitors.

How do birds fly?

Birds could not fly without feathers. Simply put, birds can fly because the air pressure on top of their wings is less than the pressure below. Birds produce this pressure by moving their wings up and down. As they do, the pressure of the air against the wing feathers lifts them. The tail feathers are used for steering and braking.

Feathers known as primary and secondary feathers are very important to the bird's flight. Both are found on the wings. The large, wing-tip primary feathers are especially important. As the bird flaps its wings, the primary feathers help control the air. They are made to change position during flight. During the wing's downstroke, the primary feathers overlap. In this position, no air can pass through them. They are then used to push against the wind.

On the contrary, during the upward movement, the feathers twist open. This allows the wind to flow between them. It is then easier for the bird to lift its wing. But to be able to stay in the air takes much effort and strength. That is why large birds prefer to soar, especially if they are traveling a long distance. This is often true of birds of prey in search of food. For soaring, the wing's back edge must be tilted down slightly. The bird must also maintain a certain speed in the air, and thereby an upward force. The same kind of force allows planes to fly. If the air is perfectly stable the bird must descend continually to maintain its speed. That is why glider planes always look for upward airstreams. There they can keep up their speed by flying in large circles.

The bird's take-off demands the greatest strength. Ducks or pigeons can take off almost vertically. Their wing muscles make up almost thirty percent of their body weight. Other ducks have rather short wings that they can use like fins under water. Because of this, they must run for a long time on the water's surface before being able to take off. Finally, very heavy birds, like the albatross, must use a "runway" for take-off. Slopes alongside their nesting grounds often meet this need.

Changes in direction are essentially directed by the tail. The tails of some birds are very small. Birds such as the swift fly very quickly. If even one feather is out of place, the birds will have trouble flying. The tail is much longer on forest birds of prey. These birds must be able to change direction quickly. Their tails make this possible.

While landing, pelicans use their webbed feet as air brakes.

Why do birds sing?

For the chaffinch (*above*) song is, above all, a warrior chant.

Bird songs have always charmed people. Many breeders of cagebirds choose their favorites based on the type of voice. In fact, from among a bird's range of sounds, two things can be distinguished: cry and song. The song is particularly developed among many small birds.

Cries are sounds made, for example, when a bird is afraid, when it finds food, etc. The song, however, has a different motivation. Still, it is sometimes difficult to tell the two apart. Certain species use noises for their song. The harmony of these sounds is not always obvious.

But in fact, what is the function of a song? Recall, if you can, the sound of the robin's song. It is heard loudest during the early morning hours on spring days. But this melody is in fact a message to the bird's neighbors. It means, "Be careful, I'm here at home. If you come here, watch out!"

For most birds, the song is one way in which the bird establishes its territory. Most birds have an area around their nest that they consider their territory. They will defend this area fiercely, especially during nesting time. That is why the robin's song is so intense during the spring. But some robins also sing in the fall. Some of these birds stay in the same nesting area all year round. (During the fall, the female robin also sings to defend its territory.)

A bird's song is often enough to frighten an intruder. Then fighting is not necessary. But sometimes a strange bird does not leave immediately. Worse yet, it may start to sing. Then, watch out! Tests have been done on this. In one example, a loudspeaker was placed near a robin's nest. The speaker projected the bird's own song. The "sweet" little bird attacked the speaker violently. It didn't stop before it had completely destroyed the machine. In another example, the speaker was placed at the limit of the bird's territory. This time, the bird was content to come and sing next to it.

The bird's song also has other roles. For example, the chaffinch uses its song to attract females to its territory. For this bird, song is a way of individual recognition. Each male chaffinch creates its own song when still young. Therefore no two chaffinches ever have exactly the same song. But like the robin, a chaffinch will not let another bird sing in its territory.

What is a bird's territory?

As you see, a bird's territory is very important. They defend it with song, and where necessary, with force. But it is interesting to see how this territory is used.

Generally, a bird's territory shelters the site where the young will be raised. Even birds that nest in colonies, like the gannet, have a territory. Gannets are large seabirds that nest in large, offshore colonies. In this case, the territory is more or less the length of the bird's neck. This is the size of space that the bird can defend without leaving its nest. But even a small space such as this is defended fiercely. Even young birds in neighboring nests are subject to the territorial rules. One who accidentally comes too close would be roughly rejected. It would be pushed from one forbidden territory to another. In some cases, it would then be pushed into the sea where it would drown.

How the nest must be built is considered when choosing a territory. For woodpeckers, the territory should include worm-eaten trees. For the titmouse, or the sittelle, it should have cavities already made.

Birds often keep their territories from one year to the next. Sometimes, however, the territory has changed from one season to the next. Even though it may no longer meet the bird's original needs, the bird will stay. Sea gulls, for example, usually nest in open spaces. Yet, in one case, sea gulls continued to nest in a dune even after trees had been planted on it.

For certain birds, the territory

also includes a hunting domain. The golden eagle, for example, prefers prey that is not easily found. To keep itself fed, it sometimes defends an area of more than 22,200 acres (9,000 hectares). The tawny owl, however, likes small rodents whose populations are always abundant. It will be happy with 50 to 500 acres (20 to 202 ha). The black woodpecker needs many worm-eaten trees. It requires 1,000 to 7,400 acres (404 to 2,995 ha).

Most smaller birds defend much smaller areas. Many of these feed on insects during the nesting season. During the winter they look for food outside their territory. Birds such as the thrush, the chaffinch, and the robin, use small areas.

For these reasons, almost all birds aggressively defend their territories. Often the intruder can be frightened away. But sometimes birds will fight to the death.

The gannet needs only a small space to make its nest. The black woodpecker defends a territory from 1000 to 7,400 acres (404 to 2,995 ha).

The battling sandpiper is one type of bird that pairs only for mating purposes.

Do birds mate for life?

Some birds, such as the Bewick's swan, choose mates for life.

Many adult birds spend a lot of time on their own. These birds form pairs only for breeding. They do not live in pairs. This is the case for pheasants or battling sandpipers, for example. These birds come together for only a short time. After mating, many males leave their "momentary" mates behind. The females then raise the young.

It is interesting to see whether these bird partners are the same from one season to the next. Of course, it is not easy to determine. This requires the expert to recognize the birds individually. He or she must be able to identify the birds after they return from their migrations. Alsacian storks, for example, always return to the same nest. It has been determined that the pairs often stay together three to four years. But they do not necessarily stay together for their whole lives.

But some birds do pair for life. This has often been observed in captive birds. Pigeons and doves are especially known for this. Some interesting studies have been done on this. One study was done on half-tamed colonies of birds known as jackdaws. These Eurasian birds, which are related to crows, usually nest in old buildings. The young jackdaws may pair off as early as the fall before their first mating season. They often stay together for their entire lives. Sometimes, a third bird will try to come between the pair. But this always causes violent quarrels.

Of all birds, geese and swans are the most faithful. Bird pairs of these types stay very close together. This is true even when the birds form large groups for migrating or hibernating.

This was studied in the Bewick's swan, which nests in northern Russia. This swan hibernates in very defined areas of northwestern Europe. One of these is the reserve of the Wildfowl Trust at Slimbridge, Great Britain. There, the ornithologist Peter Scott identified more than 1,500 Bewick's swans. An ornithologist is a scientist who studies birds. Identifying the swans was possible because of the strange yellow spots on their beaks. In almost twenty years of observations, Scott recorded only one break-up of a bird pair. Interestingly, this pair had not been able to have young.

Can birds of different species breed?

Some bird breeders love to produce hybrids. The term *hybrid* refers to the offspring of any two animals or plants of different races, breeds, varieties, etc. They are produced by a method known as crossbreeding. Some bird hybrids are very famous for their song.

But in nature, crossbreeding is rare. The reason is easy to understand. Before mating, birds perform a mating dance or ritual. The type of dance a bird does depends on the specific family to which it belongs. One specie's dance is very different from another's. The dance helps the birds recognize their mates. If either the male or female responds in a strange way, the other will lose interest.

A mating attempt between a white stork and a black stork was once observed in a zoo. The male white stork began to clack his beak. Then he placed his head upside down on his back. This is the way a male white stork tries to attract a female white stork. Seeing that, the black stork spread her tail to show the white underside. She then stretched her neck, lowered her head, and whistled. The black stork was responding with her own mating dance. But the male white stork did not understand these advances. He did not know that the female's movements were also part of a mating ritual. He soon lost interest in the black stork and went away.

In captivity, crossbreeding is easier to do. For one thing, captivity disturbs the birds' customs. They adapt their ritual gestures to the circumstances. In some cases, however, the young hybrids do not have much chance of survival. Many often die in the egg. Others, however, do survive. Some of these may not be able to reproduce. But there are exceptions to this rule. One hybrid duck, for example, has five different duck species as ancestors, Luckily for the ornithologist, this is rarely the case in the wild.

Most birds begin life as members of a family. For some of them a social life continues even after they have left their parents. These birds choose to live in large groups of their own kind. Some birds stay with the group their entire lives. Others live alone for most of the year and group together for breeding and migration. The gannet is one type of bird that gathers in huge numbers. The gannets live this way only through the mating season.

Do some birds live in societies?

The tendency of some bird species to live in large groups, or societies, is well known. It is interesting to study whether anything links the individuals living in the same group. In many bird colonies, the individuals probably know only their partners. This seems to be the case for the gannet. Gannets gather together only during the mating season. The mating season's success is determined by the colony's size. For the gannets, living in this group has just a few obligations.

But other species have elaborate social organization. For the greylag goose, for example, groups are mostly formed of family members. During the first days of existence, the chicks will become desperate if separated from their mother, brothers, or sisters. These ties continue partially afterwards. Birds coming from outside are not allowed into the group.

In most structured bird societies,

there is a hierarchy, or order by which the individuals are ranked. Among other things, these ranks determine the order in which the birds approach foods. This hierarchy can easily be observed in vultures around a carcass. High-ranking birds approach, raising their legs horizontally. The others have to wait to eat until these birds are satisfied.

But hierarchy was also studied in the jackdaws. As you remember, jackdaws mate for life. When choosing a mate, the male never chooses a female with a rank higher than his own. However, he may choose a female of a lower rank.

As for the female, she immediately takes on her mate's rank. It is possible, then, that young females may come to dominate much older birds. However, even the lowest ranking bird remains master of its own territory. The whole colony will come to its aid if it is attacked by higher-ranking jackdaws while on its nest.

The greylag goose, however, chooses to live in smaller groups. Groups are made up of mostly family members.

Do all birds migrate?

Migration is the process of moving from one area or climate to another. Birds most often migrate for feeding or breeding purposes. Migration is done at fixed times of the year along fixed routes.

A good example of migration is given by the gray cranes. Gray cranes nest in Scandinavia and in northern Russia. At the end of August they gather in northern East Germany. Then they fly over Germany and Luxembourg, reaching France in two or three big waves. They cross France's border between mid-October and early November. They may come either from the east or from the north, depending on the weather. Then they travel through France to Spain and North Africa. They return in even larger groupings in the first half of March. This is a typical example of migration.

Other birds, like the lapwings, do not migrate as such. They also move a great distance. But the movement does not follow a set pattern of date or length of travel. They are mainly directed by the weather. Lapwings always make great trips just before the freezing temperatures in France. These small waders can no longer feed when the ground becomes too hard.

The arctic tern migrates farther than any other bird. It travels about 22,000 miles (35,400 km) a year. This is the distance from its breeding grounds to its wintering grounds and back.

Finally, some species do not move at all. They are practically sedentary, or stationary. Even these birds may travel large distances occasionally when food is hard to find. They will also move if an area becomes over-populated with birds. Such is the case, for example, for domestic sparrows, or blue titmice. These birds are frequently found in the woods.

Within the same species, some birds can become migrators and others sedentary. For example, many robins in France stay in the same area the entire year. Their northern European relatives migrate to North Africa. It is the same for the well-known female ringdove. This bird crosses the Pyrenees coming from the north and the east of Europe. Male ringdoves, roosting in France, are usually sedentary.

The migration record is probably held by the arctic tern. Some nest north of the Arctic polar circle, and spend their winters south of the Antarctic polar circle. They travel down along the European and African coasts, as well as along the west coast of America. They often return along the coast of America. In all, the birds travel more than 22,000 miles (35,400 kilometers) each year.

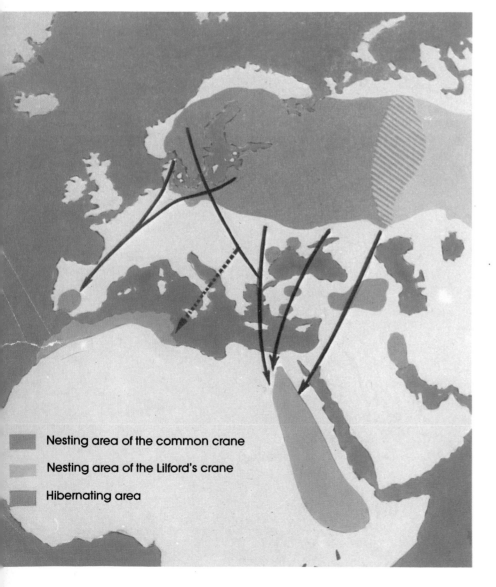

Nesting area of the common crane

Nesting area of the Lilford's crane

Hibernating area

This map compares the migration habits of the common crane to those of the Lilford's crane. Both cranes spend the warm seasons nesting in Europe. As winter sets in, they migrate to southern Europe and Africa. Notice that the birds share a certain amount of area during their nesting and hibernating periods.

The snowy owl

How long do birds live?

It is quite difficult to say how long a wild bird lives. It is impossible to watch a bird from birth until death when it lives in the wild. Experts, however, can study birds in captivity. From their findings, they can estimate the lifespan of a wild bird.

The oldest known bird on record is the great crow. One of this type of crow is known to have lived sixty-nine years in an aviary. An aviary is a place where birds are kept. A great horned owl is the next oldest at sixty-eight years. A gray gabon parrot known as Jaco lived to be fifty-nine.

But things work very differently in nature. There, many dangers threaten birds, especially when they are young. For the small sparrow in particular, many chicks die before one year of age. Many are eaten by a predator, such as a cat or larger bird. Others do not make it through winter. Still others do not survive their first migration. But, if they pass the first year, they are likely to reach five or six years of age.

The balance of life is even more striking when the titmouse or swallow is considered. A pair of these birds may raise as many as fifteen young per year. Yet their populations remain stable. In some cases, despite the high birthrate, bird populations decrease. Often, this decrease is brought on by people. The same is true of bigger, more powerful birds like ducks. For this reason, it is foolish to hunt ducks returning from migration. Those that survive migration are the strong birds. Only they can ensure the species' survival.

The technique of banding allows the identification of wild birds. In banding, birds are captured for study. Before they are released, small identification bands are strapped to their ankles. These bands will identify the birds when they are later recaptured. Banding has helped experts gather information on wild animals' lifespans.

The record to date is held by a bird known as oystercatcher, a wading bird. One of these birds was known to have lived thirty-six years after being banded.

The shelduck is one of the few birds species in which the female is more colorful than the male.

Are male birds always more colorful than the females?

In most bird species, the male is more colorful than the female. One striking example is the case of the peacock. The male peacock has a beautiful tail with superb, colorful feathers. The female has a much smaller tail. The actual number of large tail feathers is in fact different.

The male has ten; the female has eight. This difference is rather unusual.

However, in some birds there is no visible difference between the sexes. Only their behaviors set the males apart from the females. This is the case for most pigeons and doves, as well as for many parakeets and parrots. However, in this family a rather rare case is found in the king parrot. Here, both the male and the female have brilliant but different plumages. The male's is mostly green, while the female's is mostly red.

The different plumages between the sexes sometimes disappears at certain times of the year. This happens to many ducks such as mallards, teals, shovelers, pintails, etc. At the end of the mating season, the male takes on a plumage similar to the female's. This is called an eclipse plumage. It lasts through mid-fall. The eider male keeps a different plumage, but it is much less colorful at this time.

In some species, the female is less colorful but bigger than the male. This is true of many birds of prey. Then the female is also more powerful. When this happens, the female hunts more often and takes care of feeding the young. This explains why the male falcon and sparrow hawk are about one-third of the female's size.

Among the waders nesting in the northern territories, the females are often much more colorful than the males. This is also true for the painted snipe, which lives in the warm regions of Europe. In this species, pairing for life is not the rule. Instead, each female has several males to care for her during the reproduction season. This is not the case for the shelduck, from New Zealand. These birds live as very stable pairs. However, there too, the female is more colorful than the male. The young look like the male, whatever their sex. For all other ducks, the young take on the eclipse plumage of the female and the male.

Among parrots, the male and female often have identical plumages.

How many toes do birds have?

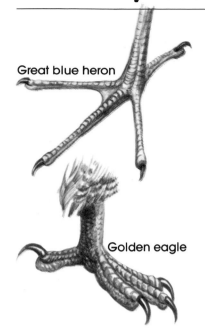

Great blue heron

Golden eagle

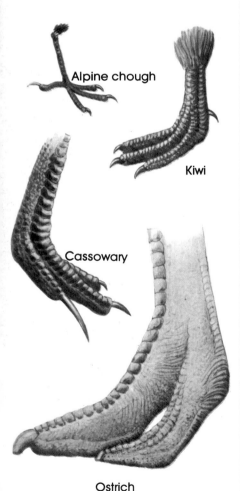

Alpine chough

Kiwi

Cassowary

Ostrich

Ornithologists can tell much about a bird simply by studying its shape. From its beak, they get an idea of the way a bird feeds. As well, the form and number of a bird's toes often tell much about its environment.

Most birds have four toes. Some birds, like pheasants and chickens, also have something called a spur. But this should not be confused with a toe. No birds are known to have five toes. But some birds do have just three toes. This is true of emus, cassowaries, and nandous. Some birds are even named for this particular feature. For example, there is the tridactyl woodpecker. The word *tridactyl* means three-toed.

Only one bird, however, is known to have two toes. This is the ostrich. Having fewer toes makes a bird faster on foot. This is very important to the ostrich, which cannot fly. Its speed allows it to outrun any predators. But such evolutionary changes also have drawbacks. Having fewer

The ostrich is the only bird known to have only two toes. Because of its foot structure, the ostrich is also one of the fastest land-running birds.

toes may mean more speed, but it also deprives a bird of its grip. This would not be good for a bird that perches or roosts.

Birds with four toes usually have one pointed backward. The other three toes point forward. The swift, however, has all four toes pointing forward. This allows this bird to get a better grasp on walls and rocks.

Woodpeckers also have specialized toes. Two of their toes point forward while the other two point backward. This allows a woodpecker to rest on the bark of trees. The position of its toes keeps the bird from slipping or falling. This is especially important to the woodpecker when it is vigorously pecking the bark. These birds are called zygodactyls. *Zygodactyl* means having two toes pointing forward and two pointing backward. But not all woodpeckers have their feet arranged this way. Parrots, however, are also zygodactyls. This allows them to hold food in their feet and bring it to their beaks. Very few birds are able to do this.

The osprey and the nocturnal, or nighttime, birds of prey are even more specialized. The fourth toe on one of these birds can be put either forward or backward at will. The most curious evolution is that of the hornbills and kingfishers. These birds have third and fourth toes that are partially connected. The reason for this is still not known.

Then there are the aquatic birds. Aquatic birds very often use their feet to swim. That is why their feet have folds of skin, or membranes, between their toes. These membranes make the birds more powerful swimmers. The moorhen has very small membranes between its

toes. Each long toe is simply bordered by a narrow strip on each side. The grebe has a strip in the form of a chestnut leaf around each of its toes. These lobes are also found on the coot. The coot, however, has a scalloped edge to its lobes.

The woodpecker is a zygodactyl. This means it can place two toes forward and two toes backward. This arrangement helps the woodpecker hold itself steady while it pecks at the tree bark.

Which birds build the most elaborate nests?

A penduline titmouse tends to its nest.

Some birds lay their eggs in very simple nests. The meadowlark will lay its eggs in a hole in the ground made by a horse's hoof. But some birds build much more elaborate nests to raise their young.

The long-tailed titmouse builds an egg-shaped nest with a side entrance. The nest is made of hundreds of feathers held together by plant fibers and spider webs. It is then disguised with a covering of moss and other vegetation. Another titmouse, known as the penduline titmouse, weaves a globe-shaped nest. It is made with fibers and grass. The bird enters its nest through a tunnel hanging from one side or below the nest. The red-rumped swallow also makes a nest with an entrance hall. But this nest is built of dry mud. It is often found hung beneath a bridge or other overhang.

But even these small works of art are nothing compared to the nests built by some exotic birds. Some swifts, especially the cave swiftlets, use their saliva to bind the building materials together. As the saliva dries, it is formed into cups. The swifts stick these cups to the walls and roofs of caves. These nests are gathered to make the famous Chinese bird's-nest soup. The best soup comes from nests made of pure saliva.

In the same style, the cayenne swift builds a vertical cylinder for its nest. The nest is open at the top and has a shelf halfway down to hold the eggs. The hedge sparrow is found mostly in Malaysia. This sparrow uses large living leaves to form its nest. The bird uses the leaves still attached to the tree. It rolls them into a cone and actually sews them together. This is done with fibers and spider webs. After that, it fills the nest with wool and hair to make it very soft.

The American orioles are also famous weavers. They build deep pouch-like nests. These nests hang from tree branches. Their entrances may be at the top or side of the nests.

Some birds build community nests. The social weaver of southern Africa builds the greatest nest of any bird. Social weavers look a lot like house sparrows and are not much bigger. Yet they build an enormous nesting house in a tree. From a distance, the nest looks like a grass hut hanging in the tree branches. Inside, there may be as many as three hundred nesting chambers. Each pair of weavers builds its own chamber and separate entrance tunnel. A huge thatched roof covers the community.

Is the nest used only for raising young?

Bird experts often receive requests for bird houses "to shelter the bird during the winter." People are always confused when they are told that few birds use the nest where they raised their young as a shelter.

Still, the nest is not only a shelter to protect the young. Its construction is part of the mating ritual. It is very important to help the bird prepare for mating. Some birds must even build several nests. The male wren, for example, makes a series of mossy nests in his territory. When the female comes, she will choose one. This nest will then be finished and become the final nest.

But the most interesting case is that of the cradle birds and the bowerbirds. These birds, which live in Australia, are very similar to the birds of paradise. The male builds a very elaborate nest. Its only purpose is to attract his mate. Later, the female will build a second nest in which the young will actually be raised.

In any case, the beauty of the "courting nest" is also important. With it, one male can successively attract several females. The brown bowerbird and the red-crested bowerbird both live in New Guinea. The attractive effect of their nests eliminates the role of plumage. Unlike their relative, the bird of paradise, the males of these species have plumage as colorless as the females!

But their nests are amazing. The brown bowerbird builds a nest, or bower, that is 3 feet (1 m) high and 4.5 feet (1.5 m) in diameter. The nest overlooks a small "garden." This garden is actually a cleared space into which the male puts flowers and other decorative objects.

The red-crested bowerbird builds a nest with very solid walls. One nest contained more than three thousand intertwined sticks and fibers. Between these, the bird puts many small pebbles. The record height is probably held by Newton's bowerbird in Australia. This bird builds a bower around the trunk of a tree. It can measure more than 9 feet (3 m) high!

The satin bowerbird and the regent bowerbird paint the edges of their nests. They use a tint made of charcoal and fruit mixed with saliva for this purpose. To spread it, the satin bowerbird uses a piece of fibrous bark. It seems to prefer the color blue, which is dominant in its plumage. This probably makes the nest more attractive to a mate.

For the bowerbirds, a courting nest attracts their mates.

How do penguins hatch their eggs on ice?

For an egg to develop normally, it must be maintained at a certain temperature. This temperature is 95° to 98.6°F (35° to 37°C), which is the temperature of the bird. Obviously, this is not easy for the Antarctic penguins. These birds must brood their eggs on the middle of the ice.

The emperor penguin breeds in the middle of the Antarctic continent. For these birds, the problem is even more complicated. Their nesting period takes place in the middle of winter. This allows the young to benefit from the short polar summer. After that they must face the diffi-culties of life alone.

In this species, the male alone incubates the eggs. The nesting, or incubation, period lasts for about sixty-four days. Afterwards, the male takes care of the newborn chick. The male fasts, living on his fat reserve for nearly three months. Leaving the egg alone for even an instant is impossible. The temperature is far below zero. Contact with the ice might also cool the egg. To avoid this, the emperor penguin lays its egg on its own feet. A thick layer of skin and fat covers it. Cornered between the feet and the belly, the egg receives all the necessary warmth for its development. The same technique is used by the king penguin. This penguin is related to the emperor penguin, but it breeds farther from the poles.

The Adélie penguins share the Antarctic continent with the emperors. To insulate the egg from the ice, they build a pile of pebbles on which to rest it. During the construction of this nest, they often steal material from one nest to place in another. This is the only way birds in the center of the colony can get enough stones for themselves. They would otherwise have to travel long distances to gather them.

Adélie penguins stay very loyal to their nests. They know how to find them again from one season to the next. This is true even when a nest is buried beneath a deep layer of snow. The male usually begins the incubation. But the female comes and replaces him. That way, the male never fasts more than six weeks. During this period, the birds are sometimes covered over with ice.

Must all eggs be incubated to hatch?

Eggs must be incubated to hatch. An embryo needs the warmth to grow and develop. Most often, the parent birds incubate the eggs by sitting on them. Rarely, as seen in the emperor penguin, the male alone

The nest of the malleefowl.

warms the egg.

But not all birds use their bodies to hatch their eggs. This is true of the birds known as megapodes. The name *megapodes* literally means "big feet." These birds are chicken-like birds of the same family as pheasants. Several species are found in wooded and open areas of Malaysia and Australia. The megapodes are interesting and unusual birds for several reasons. But above all they are unique in that they do not use their bodies to incubate their eggs. They also take no part in feeding or caring for their young.

Instead, megapodes bury their eggs in the ground. One species, known as the maleofowl, lives near the beaches. This bird buries its eggs in the sand, exactly like big sea turtles. Heated by the sun, the sand incubates the eggs. On some islands, the birds even bury their eggs next to a volcano. The hot volcanic ground incubates them.

But many megapodes use another method. These birds dig large holes in the ground. These holes are then filled with rotting leaves and other vegetation. The eggs are buried in these mounds and covered over with more vegetation and soil. Some of these piles, which the male builds, can be over 4 feet (1.5 m) high. As the pile decays, it produces heat and incubates the eggs.

Megapodes living in the brush areas are known as malleefowls. The malleefowl is the most particular of mound builders. To begin with, this bird digs a very big hole. Some measure 12 feet (3.5 m) across and 3 feet (1 m) deep. Like the other megapodes' holes, this hole is also filled with vegetable matter. The male is very much in charge of the nest building. He will not allow the female near it until the temperature is just right.

When it meets his standards, the female malleefowl may approach. She then digs a hole in the mound and lays her eggs. During the incubation period, the male continues to maintain the nest. He is especially careful about keeping the eggs at the proper temperature. To check this, he thrusts his head deep into the mound. His bill seems to serve as a thermometer. Then he will remove or add soil to maintain the proper temperature.

The work is more complex for the megapodes living in the desert regions of Australia. In the desert, it is very warm during the day and very cold at night. A megapode living there makes a pile of leaves like the brush megapodes. But this is covered over with sand. The sand will insulate the nest.

The incubation period lasts seven months. Obviously, the weather varies greatly during this period. In the spring, when the weather warms, the malleefowl digs holes into the mound. This allows air to get to the nest. But during the summer, the bird puts more sand over the nest. This protects it from the burning heat, which is much too hot for the embryos. In the fall, the male practically uncovers the eggs when the sun is warmest. He covers them again at night to store the warmth.

Finally, in the middle of the fall the chicks will hatch. They quickly dig their way through the thick layers covering them. Some chicks will die before they reach the surface. The others will emerge exhausted. They immediately run away to hide and will be able to fly within hours.

How do chicks break out of their shells?

Have you ever seen a newly-hatched chick? Looking at this weak creature, you have probably wondered how it was able to break from its shell. Breaking out of its shell takes a lot of the chick's energy. But the little bird is especially equipped for this.

During embryonic development, a special structure develops on the chick's upper beak. This small, tooth-like structure is called a diamond. Some birds, like the American sandpiper, have two diamonds.

When its development is complete, the chick begins to move about in the shell. The diamond then makes a small hole in the egg. Then the chick turns around in the egg and begins again. Soon, the chick has made a complete crown of small holes. The pressure from the chick inside is generally enough to remove the cap of the egg's largest side. The hardest work is then done. The chick has only to get out of the rest of the shell. But this is not always easy.

The parent birds do not help the chick during this operation. Their instinct has not taught them to do so. It is also the law of nature that the strongest survive. The chicks that are not strong enough to break out of their shells would probably find survival difficult, too.

How do cuckoos get other birds to raise their young?

Many people know that the cuckoo does not care for its own eggs. Its eggs and young are cared for by other birds. This habit is typical of many species of cuckoos found all over the world. It is also true of certain other birds. These include: the African widowbird, the American oriole, the honeyguide, and even the black-headed duck of South America. All of these birds are considered parasites. A parasite is an animal that depends on other animals (hosts) to survive but gives nothing in return.

Choosing an appropriate host is vital to the survival of the young. For the black-headed duck, this is no problem. It simply lays its eggs in the nests of other ducks having the same habits. It is the same for the widowbirds. These birds lay eggs in

the nests of closely-related birds known as waxbills. The chicks of the waxbills have spots in the bottoms of their throats. These spots show the host parents where to feed the young. The placement of these spots varies from one species to another. But amazingly, the widowbird chicks have the same spots. They are always placed in the same way as the spots of their hosts—whatever they may be!

The jay cuckoo lives in Africa. This bird lays its eggs in the nests of crows or magpies. In the same way, its chicks have plumages like those of the host's chicks. The gray cuckoo makes things difficult by laying its eggs in the nests of smaller birds. This cuckoo lays very small eggs for a bird of her size. The coloring of her eggs is the same as that of the host's eggs.

The young cuckoo, however, grows very quickly. It demands a great quantity of food. Its adoptive parents would be unable to feed both this piggish chick and their own offspring. The young cuckoo takes care of this problem itself. The young cuckoo always hatches some hours before the chicks of its adoptive parents. While naked and blind, the young cuckoo pushes the other eggs from the nest.

But, the honeyguides of Africa are even worse. They lay their eggs in the nests of the woodpecker and the brill. Like the cuckoo's chicks, the young honeyguides also destroy the host's brood. The honeyguides either push the others from the nest or peck them to death. The other chicks cannot survive.

How do birds protect their chicks?

During the first days of life, chicks are very fragile. Because of this they are easy prey of many larger birds. The parent birds must then protect their chicks against these birds.

For this reason, some species raise their young in well-hidden nests. They may use holes in trees, holes in the ground, or other such spots. For these birds, rodents are the danger. The wryneck, a small, brown woodpecker, uses an interesting defense against these predators. When a rodent gets near its nest, the wryneck imitates a hissing snake. Titmice are able to make the same noise by quickly beating their wings.

Some birds nest in the open. Other birds' chicks leave the nest soon after hatching. For these birds, protecting their young is a complex problem. For many of them, protecting their young means being on guard constantly. At the first sign of danger, the female duck hisses to her young. The water rail, however, carries its offspring in its beak. Sandpipers also carry their young with them. But these birds use their feet to carry the chicks.

Sea gulls and terns live together in colonies. In large groups, they will attack their enemies. Other birds, like the black-necked grebe, often nest near these colonies. Their young benefit from this form of protection.

When bothered on its nest, the owl will try to frighten its attackers. Ruffling its feathers and swelling up, it tries to look impressive. The marsh

The avocet leads predators from its nest by pretending to be wounded.

owl is especially good at this. The bird called the skua, however, will actually attack if threatened. These birds do not hesitate even if the intruder is a person. They fly at head level, dragging their feet. This causes a painful slap.

The ringed plover and the avocet have an unusual method of protection. When danger is near, the parents pretend to be injured. Some limp as if a foot is hurt. Others run along the ground with one wing hanging. Both methods draw the intruder's attention from the nest. When the "injured" bird has led the intruder a safe distance, it will fly quickly away. This action has also been seen in partridges, larks, grouse, and even some finches.

Small, shore-wading birds often lay their eggs on the beach. The eggs and chicks are sometimes attacked by larger birds. To protect their young, these birds also try to lead predators away from the nest. When there is danger, the purple sandpiper runs slyly from its nest. It gives the impression that it is a small rat.

How do birds nesting in colonies recognize their young?

Some birds are very dedicated to their young. One legend says that the pelican will tear out its entrails to feed its young. Of course the truth is different. The pelican carries fish to its young in its esophagus. There the fish are partially digested. Back at the nest, the pelican regurgitates, or throws up, the half-digested fish into its pouch. Older chicks then feed right from the pouch, burying their beaks in it. From this came the belief that the chicks eat the parent's entrails.

But pelicans are still devoted parents. As soon as they reach a certain age, the young pelicans are gathered together in "nurseries." Still, the parents will come and feed only their chick. This seems to be common among many birds that gather their chicks in nurseries. Penguin colonies have populations of several million birds. Such a large colony would need nurseries for several hundreds of thousands of young. It is amazing that the parents are able to pick out their chicks from this mass!

Gannets generally nest in smaller colonies of several thousand birds. For them, the problem is easier. Their chicks remain in the nest. The location of the nest helps the adults find their young. But if a young gannet leaves the nest, it rarely survives. It is immediately attacked by the neighbor whose territory it invades. In the end, it is thrown into the sea below.

Flamingoes also live in large colonies. Dwarf flamingoes often have several hundred thousand pairs in a colony. The young are dependent on their parents for a long time. It seems that members of the family recognize each other by voice. This explains why flamingo colonies are always so noisy.

How parents recognize their young is not always easy to answer. Some ornithologists say that Adélie penguins know their young by their facial features. But it seems that mates know each other by voice. If so, wouldn't it be the same with chicks?

It seems that at least the emperor penguins know each other by voice. The parents often "speak" to their chick before it is put in the nursery. Later, lost in the mass of other chicks, it will answer its parents' call. It is important that it be recognized by its parents. Even while it is in the nursery, they will continue to feed it.

Penguins are particularly good judges of faces.

How are young gulls fed?

Young birds require a great amount of food. Just feeding its young takes up much of a parent bird's time. The methods of feeding are varied. In some species, such as the gull, the parent regurgitates, or coughs up, food to feed the chicks.

People are often amazed at the way birds dedicate themselves to their young. They marvel at how the birds tirelessly feed the chicks. Many parents make countless trips to and from the nest to feed the hungry young. But many people do not know that the act of feeding is not voluntary. When a bird feeds its chicks, it is acting on reflex.

The act of feeding has been well studied in sea gulls. Many, like brown and silver sea gulls, have a red spot on their lower beaks. This simple spot is extremely important to the chicks' survival. When the adult bird returns to the nest with food, the chicks are waiting. The adult does not know at once to regurgitate it for them. But the chicks are attracted by the red spot on the beak. One of them starts to tap the red spot. Only then does the reflex occur in the adult. It immediately delivers the food to its young.

Several experiments were done to test this theory. Silver sea gull chicks and fake adult sea gull heads were used. The chicks paid no attention to the heads whose beaks had no red spot. But the chicks plunged at the red-spotted beaks, even if they were made from flat plywood. Heads with a completely red beak caused the same reaction from the chicks. If a rooster's comb was added to the head, this also excited the chicks. This proves that for this species, the red on the beak excites the chick to tap at the adult. In turn, the chicks' tapping causes the parent to regurgitate food.

How many chicks do owls raise?

The number of chicks a bird raises is extremely variable. Some birds, like the short-toed eagle or the gannet, raise a single chick. Others, such as the titmouse, can lay up to seventeen eggs in one brood.

The number of young a bird has depends on several things. The type, or species, of bird is of course very important. But external factors can also have a great influence. The most remarkable case is probably that of owls. The large, white owl, known as the snowy owl, is particularly interesting. For this bird, the number of eggs laid depends mainly on the food supply. The snowy owl feeds above all on small rodents called lemmings. In some years, the lemming population grows to great numbers. In other years, they are scarce.

During years when lemmings are few, very few snowy owls are born. The adult birds simply do not reproduce. But in years when lemmings are abundant, the owls can lay up to fourteen eggs per pair. This strange occurrence is also true of the barn owl. This bird nests in barns and attics. The number of eggs it lays also depends on the available food. These owls eat mostly shrews and voles. Furthermore, they begin to brood as soon as the first eggs are laid. More eggs are laid every forty-eight hours. There is often quite an age difference between the first and last chicks.

The parents always feed the chicks that are the most demanding. In a large nest, this is often the oldest chick. The younger chicks, then, suffer if there is not enough food. So the youngest do not always survive. Sometimes, they are even eaten by their siblings. This seems cruel. But it is the only way for nature to adapt the number of birds to the available food.

It also helps the strongest chicks survive in difficult times. Gray herons, for example, generally lay four or five eggs. But they can rarely raise more than three chicks. One study discovered that bird pairs in several colonies were unable to reproduce. Insecticides had harmed these birds. Despite this, the worldwide population of herons did not decrease. This was because the birds without chicks fished less. This made food more plentiful for the rest. The heron parents were able to raise all of their young.

Vultures do not have sensitive noses.

Do birds have a sense of smell?

Birds' nostrils are connected to three holes in their beaks. One of these holes is covered with cells capable of detecting odors. These cells are similar to those which are used by mammals.

These cells are linked to the brain by a special nerve. This nerve leads to the olfactory lobe located on the bird's brain. The main job of this olfactory lobe is to analyze information carried by the nerve. In some cases this structure is very sensitive. This suggests that some birds may have a sharp sense of smell. It is known that this lobe is well developed in geese, petrels, and the emus. Meanwhile, the albatross and the aura vulture have sensory organs in their nostrils. These organs can grow very big.

However, it has never been proven that odors are important to birds. For example, it was thought that vultures located dead animals by smell. These birds are known to be very good at detecting a decaying carcass from long distances. Experiments were conducted with turkey vultures. These birds have sensitive olfactory cells. These birds showed that smell alone was not enough to help them find food. They could not find decaying matter that they could not see. (For the test, the experimenters had covered the carcass with a simple layer of leaves.) Yet they sped to pieces of meat covered with prussic acid. This acid smelled very different from decaying fish.

From this, experts gather that scavengers use sight to find their food. Not much is known about sea birds, petrels, or albatrosses. These birds also have well-developed olfactory organs. But the sense of smell does seem to play an important role for the kiwi. The kiwi, which is New Zealand's national bird, cannot fly. It is also very short-sighted. But its nostrils seem to be very sensitive. They are found at the end of its long beak. They carry information about food in its path. The bird would otherwise have no way of finding it.

Do birds sleep?

Like most animals, birds need to sleep, even if they often sleep very lightly. For safety, some birds roost together. This is true of swallows. During the fall, they settle in the reeds to spend the night. It is also true for starlings or the northern chaffinch. Some of their roosts, established in shrubs, can shelter more than one million birds.

The woodpecker uses tree holes to rest in at night. These holes are not the holes in which they raised their young. Rather, they use old nests and natural holes at night. But they may also dig a place for themselves in an old tree trunk.

Nocturnal birds of prey and nightjars, of course, sleep during the day. Nightjars crouch in dead leaves on the ground. There, their plumage hides them perfectly. The owls, however, camouflage themselves against the tree trunks.

Many birds sleep perched on a branch. They have a perfected system which keeps them from falling. The tendons of their toes lock so that they stay solidly clenched on the perch. Even if the bird completely relaxes its muscles, it will not fall.

The principal concern for small birds is staying warm while sleeping. To keep warm, they puff up their feathers. This insulates the birds. The body temperature of the

The swift sleeps while flying (above).

Many perching birds can lock their feet in a closed position while sleeping.

smallest birds, like the flycatchers, still drops considerably. This causes their bodily functions to also slow down.

But the most remarkable case is that of the swifts. It is almost certain that they are able to sleep while flying! Their wings lock in a stretched out position. This and their good sense of balance keep the birds in the air.

Are snake-eating birds protected against venom?

It is well known that many birds attack snakes. Hens and guinea fowl are known to rid farms of the reptiles. For many birds of prey, snakes are a main source of food. This is the case for the secretary bird, the short-toed eagle, and the crested snake eagle of Asia.

These birds do not hesitate to attack even the most poisonous snakes. Yet, they are not protected against the venom. Only the birds' legs have some sort of protection. They are covered with tough scales that the snakes' fangs cannot pierce. But it is the speed of the bird's attack that makes survival possible.

The short-toed eagle generally begins its attack by dancing around the snake. With its wings spread wide, it tries to distract the reptile. Eventually, the snake tires and slows down its attack. The bird then spreads one of its legs. With a quick movement, it hits the snake on the back of the neck. It breaks the snake's neck with its claws. Using this technique, the juggler eagles kill the dangerous striking vipers of Africa.

The secretary bird dances in the same way. But it continually strikes the snake with its powerful feet. It generally needs only a few seconds to kill it.

Despite the bird's speed, it can happen that one is bitten and dies. But this happens very rarely. Usually, the bite does not reach the bird's flesh. The bird is protected by the plumage on its breast. In fact, a bird's head is the most vulnerable area. It has no system of protection. Only the honey buzzard has scales all around its eyes and on its face. But this bird does not attack snakes. It attacks wasps, bees, and other venomous insects. Its scales protect it from the stings of these insects.

Some birds of prey are not afraid to attack a snake—even a poisonous one. But they are not protected from the snake's venom.

Do birds of prey digest the bones of their prey?

Birds of prey generally swallow their prey whole. But their digestive juices are not strong enough to dissolve the bones and hair (or feathers). The remains form a kind of a ball in the bird's stomach. These balls, called balls of rejection, are later regurgitated. It is not known how these balls are formed. But they seem essential to the owl's proper digestion. In one example, a pygmy owl did not seem to have enough undigested matter in its system. It was seen swallowing rubber rings to regurgitate a more consistent ball.

Many of these balls are found under the bird's nest and in the general area. Their study provides ornithologists with much information about the diet of these birds. Bones are generally found in large fragments. This makes identification easy. This is especially true of nocturnal birds. These birds tend to swallow the complete skull of their prey.

But birds of prey are not the only birds to produce balls of rejection. It is also the case for most of the fishing birds. Herons, kingfishers, and some wading birds like the curlew, regurgitate pieces of shells that they swallow.

Many insect-eating birds regurgitate the indigestible parts of invertebrates that they eat. Many balls are found underneath trees which shelter colonies of rooks. Robins also reject balls. But these are very difficult to find. Even the honeyguide, which feeds on the wax of wasps' and bees' nests, regurgitates balls.

Curlews, like birds of prey, regurgitate what they cannot digest. For wading birds, it is often parts of shells.

How do diving birds see under water?

Aside from having a backbone, vertebrate animals share many features. For example, eyesight is a common feature. Vertebrates' eyes are very much like a camera. They have a system of lenses that concentrate the light rays onto a sensitive surface. This surface is known as the retina. The retina then transmits the image to the brain along the optical nerve. But such a system is designed to work in the air. Many birds' eyes do not work the same in the water.

Some birds are unable to compensate for this. Terns, for example, fish by letting themselves fall into the water from a certain height. They see their prey with precision only from the air. Once in the water, they cannot be precise. Because of this they often miss the fish.

The kingfisher feeds in the same way. It does not have a way to adapt its vision beneath the water, either. But its retina does have two foveae. A fovea is a small depression on the retina. Vision is sharpest there. Each of the kingfisher's fovea is placed in a special way. One allows underwater vision, and the other allows vision in the air.

Penguins are really adapted first for aquatic life. They have clear vision only under water. Maybe it is one of the reasons for the familiarity they often show toward people. Their short-sightedness incites them to come and take a closer look. They may be interested in this other creature that walks upright.

However, many diving birds have eyes that see as well under water as in the air. Besides two eyelids, birds have a third transparent membrane. This closes sideways. It is used to clean and to wet the eye. For the divers and the penguins, this membrane is also equipped with a lens. This lens aids underwater vision.

The kingfisher has two main focal points for each eye. This helps the bird see under water.

How do fishing birds move under water?

There are three thousand bird species known in the world. Among these, about 160 feed by completely submerging themselves. Of course, these animals have special adaptations to swim beneath the water.

The first problem comes from their weight. The birds must increase their weight to descend into the water. Only penguins are properly equipped for this. Most birds store air in their feathers. This acts as insulation. In penguins, this air has been replaced by fat, which is heavier. The other birds must compress their plumage, and get rid of the air. When the air is removed, they will be able to dive. In fact, birds have learned to control the air in their plumages. The cormorants, for example, are sometimes seen floating at the surface. At other times, only their heads and necks show above the waterline. How far they submerge depends on how much air has been compressed from the plumage.

To reach greater depths, some birds dive at high speeds and keep going. They often use their wings, too, so as not to slow down too quickly under water. This is the case of the brown pelicans, the phaetons, and the gannets. These birds

43

Birds such as gannets and pelicans use speed to dive to great depths. Once under water, they do not have much control over direction.

sometimes dive from heights of 97 to 113 feet (30 to 35 m) into the sea. Once under water, they can go only straight ahead. Penguins, puffins, and their relatives use their short wings like fins. This allows them to maneuver much better. It is the same for the cormorant. This bird uses its long, stiff tail like a rudder. In the rivers, the kingfisher chases fish by flapping its wings under water.

The performances of diving birds are remarkable. The loons, for example, can stay submerged ninety seconds or more. They dive to a depth of 39 feet (12 m). In extreme cases, loons have been known to dive as deep as 227 feet (70 m). On dives like this, the bird may stay under water for up to three minutes. It is true that a loon can last fifteen minutes under water without breathing. But it takes much strength to resist the pressure at such a depth.

Another case is that of the dipper. This bird is about the size of a blackbird. It is brown, with a white throat and a small vertical tail. To find aquatic larvae and small crustaceans, it finally found the simplest solution. It walks along the river bottom.

Do owls see at night?

Despite the legends, even owls cannot see in the darkest night. Their optical cells are no different than those in people's eyes. Optical cells are sensitive to light. But the owl's cells, like people's, need light to stimulate them. Neither human nor owl eye cells can see things in complete darkness.

But the nocturnal birds of prey do have better night vision. They can see things with about one hundred times less light than people can. For this reason, they have very big eyes. These allow the lens to concentrate a greater number of light rays onto the retina. In vertebrates, this retina is composed of two types of sensitive cells: cones and rods. Cones perceive colors and produce clear, sharp images. Rods, above all, function when light is weak. The owl's eyes, of course, have many rods.

These special adaptations to the owl's eyes also have some disadvantages. First, rods do not see colors. Because the owl's eyes have so many rods, the bird does not see colors very well. Secondly, its big eyes cannot adjust to a close object. Special feathers on the owl's face make up for this. These feathers act as another means of sense. Finally, the owl's eyes do not turn in their sockets. This forces the bird to completely turn its head to see around it.

Nevertheless, owls are able to find their prey, even if there is very little moonlight. Studies have shown that they use sound to help locate prey. Feathers that form the owl's facial disks also act as sound reflectors. They allow the owl to determine a sound's direction. Primary feathers are also an advantage. They help muffle the noise of the owl's flight.

Owls can also see in full light. They are sometimes seen hunting during the day. But this is rather rare, because then their prey sees them coming. All the advantages of a silent approach are eliminated. Furthermore, many birds, even sparrows, attack owls as soon as they see them. The only way for owls to escape these pursuers is to find shelter until night.

Owls can see well in the evening light. Their eyes are much more sensitive than people's eyes are. Owls can see with one hundred times less light.

How fast do birds fly?

It is difficult to measure the speed of a bird in flight. Some measurements have been made by following the bird with a car. Some tests have been made using radar. Still other measurements have been taken with optical instruments, such as a surveyor's theodolite.

The results of tests using these means are not always accurate. They also do not take variables into consideration. The wind, for example, cannot be taken into account. This single factor, however, plays an important role in actual speed. It can easily increase or decrease a bird's speed, especially at high altitudes.

One clever instrument does take the wind into account when measuring a bird's speed. This instrument consists of a propeller attached to a spring. The spring is stretched in relation to the resistance of the air. This system can even record the speed of some of the fastest birds. It has even measured the speed of the peregrine falcon going into a dive. This falcon was thought to be flying faster than 124 miles (200 km) an hour. In fact, the bird does not dive much faster than 80 miles (130 km) an hour.

In horizontal flight, the peregrine falcon does not fly this fast. Generally, it does not fly as quickly as the mallard. The mallard's speed can reach 63 miles (101 km) an hour. The winter teal is a little faster than this. It can fly as fast as 74 miles (120 km) an hour for short distances. The swift can fly up to 56 miles (90 km) an hour. Hummingbirds, which are among the smallest birds, can reach 45 miles (72 km) an hour. The slowest bird on record is the owl. This bird may fly only 10 to 16 miles (15 to 25 km) an hour.

Migrating birds are able to maintain these speeds for long periods of time. During competitions, for example, homing pigeons may fly as fast as 50 miles (80 km) an hour for 310 miles (500 km). But of course, these birds have been specially bred. Birds such as these are purposely bred for their speed and resistance. The process may take many generations of birds.

Tests among wild birds have also shown remarkable results. For example, the small bird known as the turnstone was captured and banded. Twenty-five hours later the bird was recaptured 510 miles (825 km) from the point of release. Similarly, a shrike traveled 434 miles (700 km) in twenty hours.

Some birds which cannot fly have become fast runners. The ostrich is known to be particularly fast. It reaches a speed of 28 miles (45 km) an hour. But this is not the record for running. The Australian emu can run up to 40 miles (64 km) an hour in short bursts. Finally, among the diving birds, the speed record for swimming goes to the penguin. It can swim as fast as 11 miles (18 km) an hour.

For such a small bird, the hummingbird flies very fast. It can reach speeds of 45 miles (72 km) an hour.

How fast do hummingbirds flap their wings?

Birds do not need to be large to accomplish remarkable feats. Indeed, even the hummingbird is remarkable in its own way. The hummingbird, for one thing, is one of the smallest birds in the world. It also has the greatest power during flight.

The hummingbird's power is due to the way it flies. Many birds glide like a plane. Hummingbirds hover like helicopters. They do this by holding their wings at an angle and completing a series of quick movements. This series of movements, which makes up one wingbeat, is amazing. At one point, the bird turns its wings completely upside down. This strange wingbeat creates an upward force. By repeating it rapidly, a hummingbird can fly forward, backward, and sideways, or hover. This movement also creates

the humming sound for which these birds are named.

Some hummingbirds may beat their wings as fast as fifty times per second. This number can reach eighty beats per second for the amethyst hummingbird of South America. Yet, this bird weighs no more than 0.1 ounces (2.8 grams). Some experts have measured even more beats per second during the mating season. During courting rituals, the birds are particularly excited. Then they may beat their wings as many as two hundred times per second.

To maintain this speed requires a lot of energy. During flight, a hummingbird uses about six times more oxygen than a sparrow does. It also needs much food. Much of its strength comes from eating nectar. Hummingbirds gather this liquid from flowers.

47

How do flamingoes feed?

There are many bird species living in the world. In studying them, ornithologists have found many methods of feeding. But one group has a method more interesting than any other group. This group is the flamingoes. Its feeding method is very like the one used by whales. It is not used by any other vertebrate. The form of the flamingo's beak is enough to get attention. It is a long, droopy bill. The flamingo holds it upside down to feed. In this position, its head is usually at least partly submerged in the water. Then it opens and closes its beak three or four times a second. As it makes these movements, the bird often wades through the water, stirring it up. With its beak, the flamingo scoops up the fine particles floating within reach. Such particles, and small blue-green algae, make up most of the flamingo's diet.

The secret to this feeding method is the flamingo's beak. The beak has fine combs along its edge. These fine combs, like the whale's baleen, act like a filter. While opening its beak, the flamingo draws back its tongue. This brings in water loaded with nutritive matter like a pump. Only the largest particles are kept outside by the combs. Then the bird closes a second filter, even tighter, by closing its jaws. It then regurgitates the water. The new filter keeps the algae inside the beak. In the whale, the baleen retain small shrimp and other shellfish.

Pink flamingoes have the least-refined filters. These flamingoes also have a more varied diet than other flamingoes. They will eat small crustaceans and other creatures in addition to the algae. A pink flamingo also usually feeds closer to the shore than the dwarf flamingo. These species share a habitat in Africa. The dwarf flamingo only eats vegetable plankton and feeds at the water's surface.

A huge quantity of algae is necessary to satisfy the flamingo's needs. A bird eats about one-tenth of its body weight each day. It has been calculated that 1,500,000 flamingoes live on Lake Nakuru in Kenya, Africa. These birds absorb about 130 tons of algae each day. Of course this algae emits spores twice daily. These spores, or reproducing cells, result in new algae. But it takes an extremely rich environment for this vegetation to grow at such a rapid rate. That is why great gatherings of flamingoes are seen only in very specific areas.

How do pelicans fish?

Some fishing birds catch fish by surprise, like herons, which lie in wait for fish. Others pursue them under water, like cormorants. However, one family is particularly well-adapted to this activity. This is the pelican family. Its members are known for the pocket of skin beneath their beaks. This skin acts as a net with which the bird fishes.

The American brown pelican still fishes by diving. The other pelicans fish only at the surface, using their pockets of skin. White pelicans often fish together in large flocks. They begin by lining themselves up on the deepest part of a lake. From there, they push the fish back toward the shallows. Then, all at once, they thrust their heads into the water. They usually come out with some large fish. These are stored in their throats before starting the process again.

There are exceptions to this fishing method. Off the Mauritania coast, for example, there is a group of small islands. This group, called the Arguin Reef, shelters an important colony of white pelicans. Many cormorants also live there. During the mating seasons of these two birds, the pelicans do not do much fishing. Instead, they live off the efforts of the cormorant. To do this, they watch the cormorants' nesting grounds. When cormorant parents come to feed their young, the pelicans attack. They strike the cormorants on the head until they disgorge part of their catch. The pelicans then take this for themselves.

Eurasian white pelicans gather together in large flocks to fish. Together, they drive fish toward the shallow water. There, they can easily be seen and captured.

Does the bearded vulture eat bone marrow?

Bone marrow from dead animals is part of the bearded vulture's diet. To get at the marrow, the bird must break the animal's bones. To do this, the vulture drops them onto rocks from the air. This shatters the bones and allows the bird to get at the marrow.

Spaniards call the bearded vulture *quebrantahuesos*. This means "bone breaker." Indeed, brains and bone marrow are a main part of this bird's diet. Like most vultures, this bird is a scavenger. That means it feeds on the dead animals it finds.

But to get at the brains and marrow, the bird must truly break bones. The technique it uses to do this is quite remarkable. Taking the bones in its claws, the vulture flies up into the air. Then it drops them from a great height onto a big rock. It then takes the nutritious matter from the bone with its tongue. The bird's tongue is especially adapted to this task.

The bearded vulture seems to use only certain rocks for this job. Or-nithologists have found some of these "anvils." Pieces of bone lay all about the rock on the ground. The bones covered a radius of 130 feet (40 m).

Sea gulls sometimes use the same method to open large shellfish. If the shell is too large to open with its beak, the gull will drop it on a rock. Some ornithologists have seen sec-retary birds using the same method to kill snakes. Usually these birds of prey kill snakes with their feet. But sometimes a bird comes across a large snake. The bird cannot kill it in the usual way. Instead, the secretary bird carries the snake into the air. The snake is then dropped from a great height onto the rocks below.

Why do some birds have large beaks?

The record for beak size is held by two groups of tropical birds, the toucans of America and the horn-bills of Europe. The toucan's beak, despite its impressive size, is very light. It is made of very rigid skin stretched over a bony structure. This makes it very solid.

The beak is very useful to the bird. With it, the bird can reach the tips of the smallest branches. There it picks the fruit on which it feeds. Because of its weight, the toucan would not be able to perch on these small branches. The beak's edges are also jagged and sharp. This makes it easier for the toucan to chew the fruit when it is hard.

But the toucan's beak also has many other uses. Some of its uses explain why the bird's beak has such bright colors. First, it is prob-ably used to attract its mate. But it can also be used to frighten away many birds of prey. Finally, the tou-can also uses its beak to frighten small birds. The toucan frightens these birds from their nests and then eats their eggs.

The structure of the hornbill's beak is very different. It is much harder than that of the toucan. In fact, it is so hard that in some coun-tries, it is carved like ivory. These hornbill carvings are, unfortunately, still made in Borneo. The "ivory" for these carvings comes from a kind of bump at the top of the hornbill's beak. This bump is not found on toucans.

The size of the hornbill's beak increases as the bird grows older. Its role seems mainly decorative. But the hornbill's beak can also cause problems. For one thing, it is very heavy. It causes the hornbill to lose balance during flight. The bird has a very long tail to compensate for this. The first two vertebrate in its backbone are also attached. This gives the bird strength and helps it support its heavy beak. Like toucans, hornbills use their beaks to pick fruits from branches. Their beaks also serve as weapons to kill small animals and even snakes.

The hornbill's beak is made of a very heavy material. It is so heavy that it throws the bird off balance during flight.

Why do parrots speak?

As you have seen, the bird's song is often used to defend its territory. Imitations, such as a parrot speaks, are a different response. In many cases, birds imitate their partner's voice to call them. This is certainly the case for parrots.

A parrot in captivity often does not have a mate. Its affections are then transferred to its owners. When the owners are absent, the bird will call them. It calls, repeating sounds it often hears them make. When the bird feels comfortable with its own-ers, it will begin to speak when they are present. It will continue to pro-nounce the same sentences.

As you can imagine, it is much more difficult to make the bird answer to a given question. When a parrot answers, it is not a real answer. Rather, it is simply perform-ing a reflex action. This action con-sists of the bird making certain sounds in response to sounds its owner makes. Most ornithologists agree that the parrots simply mimic sounds without understanding them.

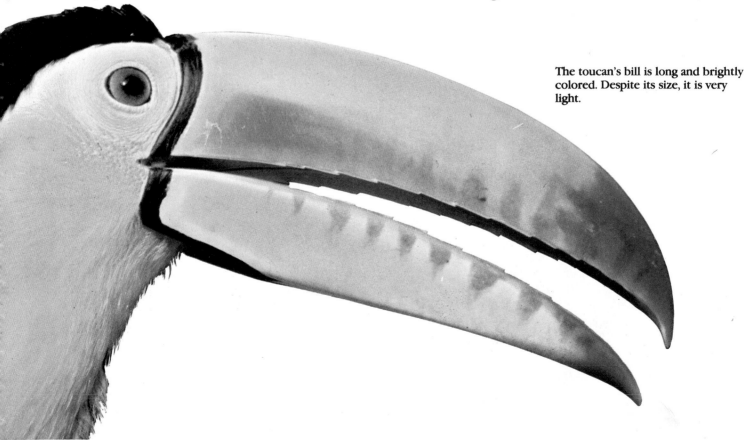

The toucan's bill is long and brightly colored. Despite its size, it is very light.

How and why do puffins dig holes?

Puffins are sea birds that live in the North Atlantic. They spend the whole winter in the middle of the sea, and come to land only to nest. Some are still found in reserves in Brittany, but pollution has reduced their numbers. But in the north, the puffins are doing well. Some small islands shelter several hundred thousand puffin pairs.

Some birds use holes dug in the ground to raise their young. Among the most well known are: petrels, shelducks, kingfishers, and bee-eaters. However, all of these birds do not dig their holes themselves. Petrels and shelducks, especially, prefer to use holes made by other animals.

The champion digger among birds is probably the monk puffin. This bird, which is also called the sea parrot, lives in colonies. The colonies nest on grassy slopes close to the sea. These slopes are soon riddled with holes in all directions. Some of the tunnels may be 16 feet (5 m) long. When the birds are present, soft purring noises come from deep within the holes.

Young birds begin to dig holes even before they are able to repro-duce. Most puffins do not lay eggs before three or four years of age. But, the young birds' holes are straight and not very deep. Adults dig the much longer holes, called galleries. There are so many galler-ies in a colony that they often cross each other. But this does not seem to bother the puffins.

The puffin digs its hole itself, using its sharp beak. Its webbed feet are also important in this process. These are used like shovels to push the soil from the hole. During con-struction, small clouds of dust are often seen coming from the holes. The hole ends in a slightly larger cavity. There the puffin lays its one egg. The same holes are used from one year to the next. But over the years, they are sometimes subdi-vided or made deeper. The oldest holes become very maze-like.

Even young puffins return to the same nesting grounds to lay their first eggs. This is an amazing event. Puffins leave the nest at six weeks of age, having rarely ventured from it. The next two years of their lives are spent on the high sea. How do they recognize the island or the cliffs of their home? Do they have some mysterious sense which leads them? The questions remain unanswered for now. But experiments are being done to find the answers.

The puffin digs a hole in which to lay its egg. Both its beak and its feet are used in this process. The beak is used like a pick to dig at the dirt. Its feet are used to push the dirt from the area.

What are the most threatened birds?

The giant, flightless dodo was first discovered in 1599. Heavy hunting and other circumstances soon caused its numbers to decline. By 1681, the dodo bird was extinct. Since that date, seventy species of birds have disappeared. Four other species are also probably extinct, although experts cannot be certain. Of this total, thirteen species were destroyed by hunting. Another fourteen became extinct when their habitats were destroyed. Eleven more were wiped out by rats, cats, and other animals introduced by civilization. Many others became extinct when other birds were brought into their territory.

The dodo is one of the most famous extinct species. The great auk is another. This bird could not fly and was an easy prey for the North Atlantic sailors. The last of these birds died in 1844. The American passenger pigeon is also now extinct. At one time, this bird was probably the most numerous on earth. Flocks of these birds still darkened the sky at the beginning of the century. They were slaughtered by hunters in such a way that they totally disappeared. The last pigeon was a captive female named Martha. She died in 1914 in the Cincinnati Zoo.

Currently, there are one hundred species of birds with less than two thousand individuals remaining. These birds are seriously threatened. With help, some of them can be saved. The American white crane, for example, numbered only fifteen birds in 1941. Since then, its nesting and hibernating areas have been heavily protected. The population

White ibis of Japan

Ivory-beaked woodpecker

has increased to fifty. Another eighteen birds are found in captivity. Experts hope that in protection, the cranes will reproduce.

The Eskimo curlew is another endangered species. These birds were once numerous in the United States. They were destroyed en masse between 1925 and 1930. In the last twenty years, the bird has been seen only rarely. It was seen six times in Texas and three times on the Atlantic coast.

Another species which may be extinct is the ivory-beaked woodpecker. This bird was last seen in 1967 in Texas, and in 1968 in Cuba. This bird often lives in large forests, where it finds insects necessary to its diet. Its decrease is linked to the systematic cutting of diseased trees. These trees are home to the insects on which the woodpecker lives.

The Eskimo curlew is an endangered bird.

The white ibis of Japan is one of the most threatened species in the eastern hemisphere. This beautiful bird was still very numerous at the beginning of the century. It was commonly found in Japan, in Korea, and in China. The transformation of the land and its cultivation has caused the bird to decline. It is no longer found on the continent. In Japan, only nine birds are known to still exist.

It is not always possible to save a species. It has been calculated that the cahow petrel may have stopped reproducing. This bird lives only on a small island in the Bermudas. It was thought extinct at the end of the seventeenth century. It was rediscovered in 1951. But, in 1958, its reproduction rate suddenly began to slow. Studies showed that insecticides had contaminated the small sea birds eaten by the petrel. No solution has been found to save this species.

The sparrow hawk maintains the health of small bird populations.

Are birds of prey harmful?

For many years, birds of prey were considered harmful. In many countries, these birds were destroyed by any means. This included both diurnal (daytime) and nocturnal (nighttime) birds of prey. The nocturnal birds were especially hunted. They were accused of bringing bad luck. In certain regions of France, they were nailed on barn doors to ward off misfortune. The diurnal birds, however, had one time been respected. Many noblemen were falconers. But the birds were accused of killing many game animals and domestic poultry. Some people even accused them of snatching sheep and small children.

Studies from the last ten years have shown birds of prey to be very useful. Experts now emphasize the need to preserve the surviving breeds from destruction. For example, the barn owl's diet is known to include rodents. In fact, small rodents such as voles, make up sixty

percent of its diet. In particularly infested regions, rodents can even make up ninety percent of the barn owl's diet.

The sparrow hawk is a small bird of prey. It also protects the fields by consuming the rodents. For this bird, rodents are seventy-two percent of its diet. Insects are another main food. Even the buzzard eats a great amount of rodents. Its diet consists of fifty-seven percent rodents. Insects and snakes make up another thirty-three percent. Smaller poultry and game birds represent only six percent of their prey. These birds are obviously more helpful than harmful.

At first, the cause of species like the goshawk and the sparrow hawk seems more difficult to plead. The goshawk's diet includes about forty percent pigeons, ten percent game

birds, etc. About seventy-eight percent of the sparrow hawk's diet is small birds. A more extensive study shows that even these birds are helpful. Compare its methods to a buzzard's. A buzzard lies in wait for its game. It captures voles, for example, whether they are healthy or not. The goshawk and the sparrow hawk must pursue their prey. They are often unsuccessful. In other words, a bird in good health has a good chance of escaping. Those that are sick or handicapped will surely be caught.

This may seem cruel. But you must remember that there is no veterinary service in nature. This process is the only way to keep a bird species healthy. So it is important that birds of prey are protected. Laws protecting them must be respected.

The sparrow hawk is an untiring destroyer of rodents.

Birds are found throughout the world in all sorts of environments. These range from the grassy plains of Africa to the icy regions of the South Pole.

Where are birds the most abundant?

People are often astonished by the way birds nest. In some areas, the density of birds is very high. Not far away, nothing sings nor flies.

The reason is that birds need areas where vegetation is varied. The nutrients that a plant provides are generally good only for a certain period of time. During other periods, they will need other vegetation to survive. A well-cleared pine forest, for example, shelters a very limited number of species. But the number of species will increase if new tree types are introduced. Encouraging brush and other plants to grow beneath the trees will also increase the bird species in the area.

In the same way, insect-eating birds cannot live all year on insects. During winter, these insects will take the form of larvae. Then they will only be found buried in the ground. During this season, birds have to eat food that they find in bushes or at the edges of woods. In Russia, hedges were planted along the edges of steppes. This increased the species of nesting birds from fourteen to seventy! Generally, forest edges are always more populated than the forest itself, or the plains next to it.

Coastal areas mix land and water elements. These areas can also be very rich in bird life. This is especially true of coastal estuaries. There, silt deposits added to the plankton allow for the development of many life forms. Such areas are generally able to feed many birds in any season. They provide for a greater density of birds than most other environments.

Are insect-eating birds really useful?

In 1902, a number of European countries signed an agreement calling "for the protection of birds useful for agriculture." This phrase often makes the supporters of industrialized culture laugh. They think that most birds are no longer numerous enough to affect insect populations. Studies made in Germany, Great Britain, and Russia show otherwise.

In Russia, insect-controlling methods are well organized. One calls for school children to put up bird houses. Russian ornithologists calculated that a titmouse has to consume its own weight in food every day. Then, one brood of titmice is enough to control the parasites on forty apple trees.

In southern Russia, locusts are still a great agricultural problem. Periodic invasions of the insect destroy everything in their path. The starlings are very efficient against them. In one month, one thousand starlings can destroy twenty-two tons of locusts. But the record is probably held by a colony of sea gulls, on the coast of the Black Sea. In 1931, cotton was introduced to the Ukraine. Cotton is a favorite food of many caterpillars. Caterpillars immediately became a prob-

Some birds are actually an important key to insect-control methods.

lem, causing widespread damage to the cotton crop. A nearby colony of gulls was then entering its nesting period. This colony of 12,500 gulls destroyed 225 tons of caterpillars.

Bullfinches sometimes damage orchards by eating the buds from the trees.

This amount is equal to the load of fourteen railroad cars!

Another very harmful butterfly in gardens is the rape pierid. The caterpillars of this butterfly attack many garden vegetables. But it has been shown that for every one hundred caterpillars, only ten arrived at the adult stage. The other ninety died. Eighty died of various causes at early stages. The last ten were destroyed by birds. Birds always choose large, strong caterpillars. These caterpillars are at a stage where they are no longer threatened by other things. So, the birds' role is very important. Without birds, the number of butterflies reaching the reproduction stage would immediately double.

Are birds harmful to cultivation?

Many insect-eating birds should be considered useful to agriculture. But many of these same birds also eat grains and fruits. These eating habits cause problems.

During the nesting season, many birds are insect-eaters. Birds such as sparrows, linnets, goldfinches, etc., need the rich insect diet to raise their young. These same birds, however, can later be harmful to fields and gardens.

This problem is the result of the modern farming methods. To make the use of the machines easier, the same cereals or the same fruit trees are planted over huge surfaces. In the past, crops were also mixed. Also, these crops were frequently rotated.

Nowadays, a fruit- or seed-eating bird can find most crops in great quantities. When a bird finds a plant it likes, it is sure to find an endless supply. It will reproduce quickly when food is unlimited. This is the case, for example, of the camargue sparrow. The development of rice as a crop gave this bird unlimited food.

This does not mean that these birds should be destroyed. Rather, today's single-crop farming methods may not be the answer. Birds are among the least harmful pests. Yet because of the same idea, many harmful insects and rodents reproduce quickly, too.

Are certain birds dangerous to people?

You may have heard stories about eagles, bearded vultures, or other birds carrying off children. However few birds are at all dangerous to people.

Eagles cannot carry much more than their own weight into the air. Female eagles are larger than males. Yet even a large female does not weigh nearly what a person does. Also, eagles are far too afraid of people to approach them. Anyone who has ever tried to photograph wild eagles knows this.

Of course, many birds may attack if their young are threatened. Large birds such as skuas (birds of polar regions of the gull family), owls, or other birds of prey may make violent attacks. They will strike out with beaks and claws. One English photographer found this to be true when he came too close to an owl's nest. Other birds, such as the tern, will dive on predators.

Even a swan will attack anyone who threatens its nest. With powerful strikes of its wings, it will try to drive the intruder away. But this is more true of domesticated birds that have lost their fear of people. Wild swans still tend to flee.

But most birds are too small and weak to make much of an attack on their own. For this reason, many birds live in groups. Then the flock bands together to drive off enemies.

The only mortal bird attacks are sure to have been due to ostriches and cassowaries. One strike from the large feet of these birds could gore a person. Such accidents sometimes happen in New Guinea. There the cassowaries are raised in villages. But again, these are domesticated birds. Wild birds rarely attack. A wild bird's first reflex is to flee.

The cassowary becomes dangerous only in captivity. Domesticated birds lose their fear of people. These birds are more likely to strike when threatened than are wild birds. Wild birds tend to flee.

How can people help birds?

As you have seen, many bird species are in danger of extinction. At the very least, many bird populations are decreasing in a disturbing way. What can people do to help them survive?

Actually saving a species at the edge of extinction is a matter for specialists. They have both the training and knowledge. But individuals can help by contributing to groups that finance these specialists. The World Wildlife Fund is one such group. Many countries also have their own organizations for this purpose.

Still, there are ways that everyone can help. Today, even the common species are finding it more and more difficult to survive. As the world becomes more full of concrete and steel, for example, birds have trouble finding nesting areas. People can help by putting up artificial birdhouses for them. Placed correctly, birdhouses are soon occupied.

Birds also have trouble finding the proper foods to eat. Today, many hedges are leveled. Weeds are quickly exterminated. Both of these are important food sources for birds during the winter. For this reason, it is good to put out seeds and fats during the winter. But it is important to continue this feeding until spring. Only then is food once again easy to find. But until then, birds will be confused if they find an empty feeder. It is also important to put the feeder in a safe place. It must be out of the reach of cats and other bird predators.

Above all, it is important for birds to have quiet areas. They need places where they will not be chased or bothered. They need to be able to reproduce in peace. Creating such reservations and refuges for birds is still one of the best answers.

What is banding?

Banding is one method of identifying birds. It consists of marking a bird with a light metallic ring. Generally the ring is placed around the bird's leg. But sometimes it is also placed around the bird's neck or wings. This ring, or band, has numbers on it which identify the bird.

Originally, banding was used to study the bird's migrations. But today the information is used in a variety of ways. For one, it is also a means of studying the lifespan of birds in the wild. And, of course, banding allows experts to calculate the number of birds living in a region. Suppose that in a given territory one hundred birds of a particular species were banded in one day. Eight days later, the banding is done again. This day, one hundred of the same birds are captured. Ten of these birds are already banded. From this, experts determine the total number of that type of bird found in the area. In this case, ten percent of the total was captured the first time. Thus there are one thousand of that species in the studied area.

(Above) A group of ducks find themselves trapped. These ducks will be banded and registered before they are released.

Each banded bird is given a number which identifies it. This number, along with information about the bird, is kept on record.

(Above) A band is a small, metal tab that identifies a bird. Usually, the band is attached to the bird's leg. Placed there, it causes the bird no problem.

Glossary

adapt to adjust to new environments or situations.

algae a group of mainly aquatic (water) plants without true stems, roots, or leaves, but containing chlorophyll. Seaweed is one type of alga.

balls of rejection small masses of matter that a bird swallows but cannot digest. This matter, which includes things such as bones, feathers, and fur, forms small balls in a bird's stomach. These balls are later regurgitated.

barb any of the side branches of the shaft of the feather. Barbs branch out from the feather's shaft like the branches on a tree. All the barbs together form the vane.

barbules the hundreds of tiny barbs that branch out from each barb. Barbules are covered with hooklets that interlock with those on other barbules. The barbules and their hooklets give the feather a smooth, even appearance.

brood the young, as of a bird or insect, hatched or cared for at one time. Brood can also refer to the actual act of sitting on and warming eggs.

camouflage to hide by blending with the environment.

carcass a dead body, especially of a slaughtered animal.

chlorophyll any of a group of pigments found in green plants.

colony a large group of birds which live together and depend on each other for survival.

cones light-sensitive cells in the eye that allow one to see colors and sharp detail, especially in bright light.

contour feathers one of the main kinds of feathers covering a bird's body. Bird feathers are basically either contour feathers or down. Contour feathers cover the wing, body, and

tail of the bird. They are known for their fern-like shape.

diurnal birds birds that are active during the daytime.

down one of the main kinds of feathers on a bird's body. A down feather is a small, soft feather found beneath the contour feathers. It has no central shaft; its fibers grow outward from a common center.

fovea a small depression in the back of the eyeball. In the fovea, the layer of nerve cells over the cones is very thin. This makes the fovea the area of sharpest vision in the eye.

hierarchy an order within a group by which the individuals are ranked. In bird groups, hierarchy often determines the order in which the birds approach food, which birds may mate with which birds, etc.

hooklets the tiny hooks of a barbule. Hooklets interlock with those on other barbules, giving the feather a smooth appearance.

host an animal or plant which provides for a parasite. The host may provide food, lodging, or both depending on the type of host and parasite.

hybrid the offspring of two animals or plants of different breeds, varieties, or species.

incubation period the length of time it takes for eggs to hatch. During this time, the parent bird must sit on the eggs and warm them with its body heat. Incubation periods vary. Some eggs hatch in as little as twelve days; others may take sixty or more days.

intermediary feathers feathers found between the down and the contour feathers. Intermediary feathers have tips like contour feathers and bases like down.

mating season specific times of the year in which animals come together to breed.

melanin a dark brown or black pigment found in both animals and plants.

migration the act of moving from one region or climate to another at specific times of the year, usually for mating or feeding purposes.

molt to shed hair, feathers, shells or other outer layers.

nocturnal birds birds that are active during the night.

optical cells cells within the eyes that are sensitive to light. Vertebrates have two types of light-sensitive cells: rods and cones (*see* rods and cones).

ornithologist one who studies birds.

ornithology a branch of zoology dealing with birds.

parasite an animal that depends on other animals to survive but gives nothing in return.

plankton drifting masses of tiny plant and animal life in a body of water.

predator an animal that hunts and kills other animals for food.

preening gland (*see* uropygial gland).

primary feathers those feathers of a bird that are used for flying. The primary feathers connect to bones on the bird's wings that correspond to a person's hand.

quill the hollow barrel of a feather. Certain feathers of a bird's plumage are also known as quill feathers. These are the large stiff feathers of the tail or wing.

rachis the upper part of the feather's shaft. The rachis supports the flat part of the feather, which is known as the web or vane.

regurgitate to throw up partially digested food. Some birds feed their young by regurgitation.

rods light-sensitive cells in the eye that allow one to see in dim light. Rods are not sensitive to color.

scavenger an animal that feeds on dead or decaying animal matter.

secondary feathers feathers of a bird's wing that are important to flight. The secondary feathers are attached to bones that correspond to a person's forearms.

species a group of animals which scientists have identified as having common traits.

spore a simple reproductive cell found in non-flowering plants and certain lower animals.

spur a sharp, pointed attachment found on the legs of some birds.

uropygial gland an oil-producing gland found at the base of a bird's tail. The bird uses oil from this gland to smooth and waterproof its feathers. The uropygial gland is sometimes called the preening gland.

vibrissae bristly, moustache-like feathers surrounding the mouths of many birds. The vibrissae feathers act like a sense organ, giving the bird an extra "sense of touch." In many insect-eating birds, these feathers can prevent insects from escaping.

INDEX